PART I

Thoughts for Mothers

"The wisdom of the wise
and the experience of the ages
may be preserved by quotations."
-Isaac D'Israeli

Motherhood

The bravest battle that ever was fought -
Shall I tell you where and when?
On the maps of the world you will find it not:
It was fought by the Mothers of Men.
Not with cannon or battle shot,
With sword or nobler pen;
Not with eloquent word or thought
From the wonderful minds of men;
But deep in a walled-up woman's heart;
A woman that would not yield;
But bravely and patiently bore her part;
Lo! there is the battlefield.

Joaquin Miller

For Mothers

CONTENTS

"For the mother is and must be, whether she knows it or not, the greatest, strongest and most lasting teacher her children have."

Hannah Whitall Smith

The mother's love -- there's none so pure,
So constant, and so kind;
No human passion doth endure
Like this within the mind.

Anonymous

"Mother's love grows by giving."

Charles Lamb

When God thought of mother,
He must have laughed with satisfaction
And framed it quickly --
So rich, so deep, so divine, so full of soul,
Power, and beauty was the conception.

Henry Ward Beecher

Only One Mother

Hundreds of stars in the pretty sky,
Hundreds of shells on the shore together
Hundreds of birds that go singing by,
Hundreds of bees in the sunny weather.
Hundreds of dew drops to greet the dawn,
Hundreds of lambs in the purple clover,
Hundreds of butterflies on the lawn,
But only one mother the wide world over.

George Cooper

"For me, a line from my mother is more efficacious than all the homilies preached ... "

Henry Wadsworth Longfellow

She broke the bread into two fragments and gave them to the children, who ate with avidity. "She hath kept none for herself," grumbled the Sergeant. "Because she is not hungry," said a soldier. "Because she is a mother," said the Sergeant.

Victor Hugo

"The future destiny of the child is always the work of the mother."
Napoleon

"All that I am my mother made me."
John Quincy Adams

"All I am or hope to be, I owe to my angel mother ... I remember my mother's prayers and they have always followed me. They have clung to me all my life."
Abraham Lincoln

"All that I have ever accomplished in my life, I owe to my mother."
Dwight L. Moody

"All I am I owe to my mother ... I attribute all my success in life to the moral, intellectual, and physical education I received from her."
George Washington

"My mother was the source from which I derived the guiding principles of my life."
John Wesley

"The mother or father who harvests thorns should look to his or her gardening. Children respond to steadfast love like a plant in the sunshine, sprouting new dimensions to his or her personality on the side where the sun shines brightest."

Author Unknown

The glory of every mother we can see,
As she holds her wee baby on mother's knee,
And so molds the fate of this old World,
More than forts, armies and flags unfurled.

William H. Morgan

"Mothers ... fill places so great that there isn't an angel in heaven who wouldn't be glad to give a bushel of diamonds to come down here and take their place."

Billy Sunday

"Children are what the mothers are."

Walter Savage Landor

"In all my efforts to learn to read, my mother shared fully my ambition and sympathized with me and aided me in every way she could. If I have done anything in life worth attention, I feel sure that I inherited the disposition from my mother."

Booker T. Washington

They say that man is mighty,
He governs land and sea,
He wields a mighty scepter
O'er lesser powers that be,
But a mightier power and stronger
Man from his throne has hurled,
For the hand that rocks the cradle
Is the hand that rules the world.

William Wallace

"The mother's heart is the child's schoolroom."
Henry Ward Beecher

Prayer

"If we believe that God is always at hand, always ready to hear, surely we should take delight in telling Him all our little cares, and woes, and hopes, as they flit by."

H. L. Sidney Lear

I know not by what methods rare,
But this I know: God answers prayer.
I know not if the blessing sought
Will come in just the guise I thought.
I leave my prayer to Him alone
Whose will is wiser than my own.
Eliza M. Hickok

"Just as in prayer it is not we who momentarily catch His attention, but He ours, so when we fail to hear His voice, it is not because He is not speaking so much as that we are not listening ... God has special confidences for each soul. Indeed, it would seem as though the deepest truths came only in moments of profound devotional silence and contemplation."
Charles H. Brent

"There is always time to look up to Him for His smile."

F. B. Meyer

"It is small things that, just because of their smallness, distress and overset us. I mean the weight of daily care, which in their small details of personal expenditure, and in the careful routine of a household, and in the rearing of children, and in the society of friends, and in the outside duty, and in private affairs, singly and separately is sufficiently burdensome; but altogether, and on one set of shoulders, is sometimes felt to be more than the strength can bear ... Where there is prayer, there is peace; and God, who makes every duty possible, knows, helps, and cares."

Anthony W. Thorold

More things are wrought by prayer
Than this world dreams of.
Wherefore let thy voice
Rise like a fountain for me night and day ...
For so the whole round earth is every way
Bound by gold chains about the feet of God.
Alfred, Lord Tennyson

Relationships

"Do not make life hard to any."
Ralph Waldo Emerson

Should you feel inclined to censure
Faults you may in others view
Ask your own heart, ere you venture,
If that has not failings, too.
Let not friendly vows be broken,
Rather strive a friend to gain.
Many a word in anger spoken
Finds its passage home again.
Do not, then, in idle pleasure
Trifle with another's fame.
Guard it as a valued treasure,
Sacred as your own good name.
Do not form opinions blindly;
Hastiness to trouble tends.
Those of whom we thought unkindly
Oft become our warmest friends.

Author Unknown

"No one has it so good but that two or three
words can dishearten, and there is no calamity
but a few right words can hearten."

Author Unknown

"Look around you, first in your own family, then among your friends and neighbors, and see whether there be not some one whose little burden you can't lighten, whose little cares you may lessen, whose little pleasures you can promote, whose little wants and wishes you can gratify. Giving up cheerfully our own occupations to attend to others, is one of the little kindnesses and self-denials. Doing little things that nobody likes to do, but which must be done by someone, is another. It may seem to many, that if they avoid little unkindnesses, they must necessarily be doing all that is right to their family and friends; but it is not enough to abstain from sharp words, sneering tones, petty contradiction, or daily little selfish cares; we must be active and earnest in kindness, not merely passive and inoffensive."

Little Things, 1852

"To cultivate kindness is a great part of the business of life." Samuel Johnson

Tell not abroad another's faults
Till thou hast cured thine own;
Nor whisper of thy neighbor's sin
Till thou art perfect grown.

Lyra Mystica

"There are often bound to us, in the closest intimacy of social or family ties, natures hard and ungenial, with whom sympathy is impossible, and whose daily presence necessitates a constant conflict with an adverse influence ... Can we bear with them in love? Can we avoid harsh judgments, and harsh speech, and the making known to others our annoyance? The examination will probably teach us to feel the infinite distance between us and our divine Ideal, and change censoriousness of others into prayer for ourselves."

Harriet Beecher Stowe

"And yet, let a man make a beginning, and all will be well. Let him steadily set himself to behave towards those whom he employs, or those who employ him, towards railway porters and shop assistants and others who minister to his convenience, as being men and women with the same right to courteous treatment, and to a real opportunity to make the best of themselves, as he has himself; let him thus realize his debts to his nearest 'neighbors,' and the whole idea of humanity, of brotherhood, will be deepened and made real to him. He will get a habit of consideration and thoughtfulness for others, as belonging to Christ, which will express itself habitually towards all, and especially the weak."

Charles Gore

"The habit of expressing appreciation is oil on troubled waters. Fortunately, it is a habit that can be formed by anyone who will take the trouble."

Trust

He knows, He loves, He cares --
Nothing this thought can dim;
Only the best He gives to those
Who leave the choice with Him.

Author Unknown

Build a little fence of trust
Around today.
Fill the space with loving work,
And therein stay.
Look not through the sheltering bars
Upon tomorrow;
God will help you bear what comes
Of joy or sorrow.

Mary Frances Butts

"Strive to be as a little child who, while its mother holds its hand, goes on fearlessly and is not disturbed because it stumbles and trips in its weakness. So long as God holds you up by the will and determination to serve Him with which He inspires you, go on boldly and do not be frightened at your little checks and falls, so long as you can throw yourself into His arms in trusting love. Go there with an open, joyful heart as often as possible; if not always joyful, at least go with a brave and faithful heart."

St. Francis DeSales

"I find that while faith is steady nothing can disquiet me, and when faith totters nothing can establish me ... Keep close to God and then you need fear nothing."   Joseph Eliot, 1664

I saw a little child, with bandaged eyes,
Put up its hands to feel its mother's face;
She bent, and took the tender groping palms,
And pressed them to her lips a little space.
I know a soul made blind by its desire,
And yet its faith keeps feeling for God's face --
Bend down, O Mighty Love, and let that faith
One little moment touch thy lips of Grace.
                                        Anna J. Grannis

"This is believing indeed; the rolling all our desires and burdens over upon an almighty God; and where this is, it cannot help but establish the heart in the midst of troubles, and give it a calm within in the midst of the greatest storms."
                                        Robert Leighton

"Do not fear circumstances. They cannot hurt us, if we hold fast to God and use them as the voices and ministries of His will. Trust Him about every one and everything, for all times and all needs, earth and heaven, friends and children, the conquest of sin, the growth of holiness ... "

Anthony W. Thorold

"Thoughts that disturb and trouble us seldom come from God. It is generally best to put them away, and throw ourselves, with increased trust in Him and mistrust of self, at His feet. And never forget, amid whatever may befall you, -- dryness, coldness, desolation, and disappointment, consciousness of many faults, and of great weakness, and lack of faith, -- that where love is, there God is sure to be. He never yet has suffered any soul to fall wholly from Him which, amid all its frailties and falls, clings to Him in love."

H. L. Sidney Lear

Just to trust Him, this is all!
Then the day will surely be
Peaceful, whatso'er befall,
Bright and blessed, calm and free.

Frances R. Havergal

"You have trusted Him in a few things, and He has not failed you. Trust Him now for everything, and see if He does not do for you exceeding abundantly above all that you could ever have asked or thought, not according to your power or capacity, but according to His own mighty power, that will work in you all the good pleasure of His most blessed will. You find no difficulty in trusting the Lord with the management of the universe and all the outward creation, and can your case be any more complex or difficult than these, that you need to be anxious or troubled about His management of it?"

Hannah Whitall Smith

Family

"The spirit of a household reaches farther than from the front door to the back. It shines forth from a child's eyes and shows in the way a man hurries back to his home."

Author Unknown

"The real empire is at the fireside."
                                        Cicero

"If things go well with the family, life is worth living; when the family falters, life falls apart."
                                        Michael Novak

A house is built of logs and stone,
Of tiles and posts and piers,
A home is built of loving deeds
That stand a thousand years.
                                        Victor Hugo

"Loving relationships are a family's best protection against the challenges of the world."
                                        Bernie Wiebe

"Children have more need of models than of critics."
                                        Joseph Joubert

"Religious words have value to the child only as experience in the home gives them meaning."
John Drescher

There's one sad truth in life I've found,
While journeying east to west;
The only folks we really wound
Are those we love the best.
We flatter those we scarcely know;
We please the fleeting guest,
And deal full many a thoughtless blow
To those who love us best.
Author Unknown

"Childhood is like a mirror, which reflects in afterlife the images first presented to it."
Samuel Smiles

"I value this delicious home feeling as one of the choicest gifts a parent can bestow."
Washington Irving

Beauty

The year's at the spring,
And day's at the morn;
Morning's at seven;
The hillside's dew-pearled;
The lark's on the wing;
The snail's on the thorn;
God's in His heaven --
All's right with the world.
                    Robert Browning

All things bright and beautiful,
All creatures great and small,
All things wise and wonderful --
The Lord God made them all.
The purple-headed mountain,
The river running by,
The morning, and the sunset
That lighteth up the sky.
He gave us eyes to see them,
And lips that we might tell
How great is God Almighty,
Who hath made all things well.

From 'All Things Beautiful'
by Cecil Francis Alexander

Compensation

The sweet-voiced nightingale is dusky brown,
While golden-plumaged birds no music own.
The ruby long outlives the scented rose;
But then the ruby no such fragrance knows.

Archbishop Richard Chenevix Trench

Love

"Love knows no limit to its endurance, no end to its trust, no fading of its hope; it can outlast any-thing. Love still stands when all else has fallen."

Author Unknown

"We love ourselves notwithstanding our faults, and we ought to love our friends in like manner."

Author Unknown

"Love never reasons but profusely gives, gives like a thoughtless prodigal its all, and trembles then lest it has done too little."

For we must share, if we would keep,
That good thing from above;
Ceasing to give, we cease to have --
Such is the law of Love.

Archbishop Richard Chenevix Trench

"This is the miracle that happens every time to those who really love ... the more they give, the more they possess of that precious nourishing love from which flowers and children have their strength, and which could help all human beings if they would take it without doubting."

Rainer Maria Rilke

"Be persuaded, timid soul, that he has loved you too much to cease loving you."

Francois De La Mothe Fenelon

Let your love be wide as His,
With the whole world around His knees;
Gather into your warm heart
All His creatures, -- not a part;
So your love shall be like His.

Katharine Tynan Hinkson

"The most trivial action may be performed to ourselves, or performed to God. If love be in your heart, your whole life may be one continual exercise of it. Oh, if we did but love others! How easily the least thing, the shutting of a door gently, the walking softly, speaking low, not making a noise, or the choice of a seat, so as to leave the most convenient to others, might become occasions of its exercise."

Mere Angelique Arnauld

Forgiveness

"Are you willing to be made willing to forgive?"
Author Unknown

"He who has not forgiven an enemy has never yet tasted one of the most sublime enjoyments of life."

Author Unknown

Has some resentment
wrought strife and ill-will?
Love and forgiveness
work miracles still.

Author Unknown

"Hatred is like an acid. It can do more damage to the vessel in which it is stored than to the object on which it is poured."

Author Unknown

"The remedy for wrongs is to forget them."

Author Unknown

"Of him that hopes to be forgiven it is required that he forgive."

Author Unknown

"We cannot give like God, but surely we may forgive like Him."

Author Unknown

"When a person forgives another, he is promising to do three things about the intended wrongdoing: not to use it against the wrongdoer in the future; not to talk about it to others; and not to dwell on it himself."

Jay Adams

"The hatred we bear our enemies injures their happiness less than our own."

Author Unknown

"Hate is sand in the machinery of life ... love is oil."

Author Unknown

"Hate is spiritual suicide."

Author Unknown

Living

"There is only one thing for us to do, and that is to do our level best right where we are, every day of our lives; to use our best judgments, and then to trust the rest to that Power which holds the focus of the universe in His hands and which doeth all things well."

O.S. Marsden

"One thing is indisputable: the chronic mood of looking longingly at what we have not, or thankfully at what we have, shows two very different types of character. And we certainly can encourage the one or the other in ourselves."

Lucy C. Smith

There's a law that I am learning
That is helping me each day:
That our Lord sends something better
For each thing He takes away.

Author Unknown

"God never wastes anything. God never forgets anything. God never loses anything. As long as we live we have a work to do. We shall never be too old for it, nor too feeble. Illness, weakness, fatigue, sorrow, -- none of these things can excuse us from this work of ours. That we are alive to-day is proof positive that God has something for us to do to-day."

Anna R. B. Lindsay

"What can be more unkind than to communicate our low spirits to others, to go about the world poisoning the fountains of joy? Have I more light because I have managed to involve those I love in the same gloom as myself? Is it not pleasant to see the sun shining on the mountains, even though we have none of it down in our valley? Oh, the littleness of that sickly appetite for sympathy, which will not let us keep our sorrows to ourselves! Let us hide our pains and sorrows. But, while we hide them, let them also be spurs within us to urge us on to all manner of overflowing kindness and sunny humor to those around us. When the very darkness within us creates a sunshine around us, then has the spirit of Jesus taken possession of our souls."

Frederick W. M. Faber

"No one can be good to others without being good to himself."

"Remember that your work comes only moment by moment, and as surely as God calls you to work, He gives the strength to do it. Do not think in the morning, 'How shall I go through this day? I have such-and-such work to do, and person to see, and I have not strength for it.' No, you have not, for you do not need it. Each moment, as you need it, the strength will come, only do not look forward an hour; circumstances may be very different from what you expect. At any rate you will be borne through each needful and right thing 'on eagles' wings.' Do not worry yourself with misgivings; take each thing quietly."

Priscilla Maurice

"God does not demand impossibilities."

St. Augustine

"Our grand business in life is not to see what lies dimly at a distance, but to do what lies clearly at hand."

Attitude

"Happiness or unhappiness depends
more on the way we meet events
than on the nature of those events themselves."

Criticism
A good thing to remember
And a better thing to do
To work with the construction gang
And not with the wrecking crew.

"Not just live and let live, but live and help live."

"Forgive us if this day we have done or said anything to increase the pain of the world. Pardon the unkind word, the impatient gesture, the hard and selfish deed, the failure to show sympathy and kindly help where we had the opportunity, but missed it; and enable us so to live that we may daily do something to lessen the tide of human sorrow, and add to the sum of human happiness."

F. B. Meyer

"A cheerful friend is like a sunny day."

"It would seem as if very few of us give this power of kind words the consideration which is due to it ... Nevertheless, with the help of grace, the habit of saying kind words is very quickly formed, and when once formed, it is not speedily lost. Sharpness, bitterness, sarcasm, acute observation, divination of motives, -- all these things disappear when a man is earnestly conforming himself to the image of Christ Jesus. The very attempt to be like our dearest Lord is already a well-spring of sweetness within us, flowing with an easy grace over all who come within our reach."

Frederick William Faber

If you hear a kind word spoken
Of some worthy soul you know,
It may fill his heart with sunshine
If you only tell him so.

Author Unknown

Every day is a fresh beginning;
Listen, my soul, to the glad refrain,
And spite of old sorrow and older sinning,
And puzzles forecasted and possible pain,
Take heart with the day, and begin again.
Susan Coolidge

"He enjoys much who is thankful for little."

"We see always what we are looking for, and if
our mind has become trained to look for
trouble and difficulty and all dark and dreary
things, we find just what we seek. On the other
hand, it is quite as easy to form the habit of
looking always for beauty, for good, for
happiness, for gladness, and here, too, we shall
find precisely what we seek."
J.R. Miller

"Seek to cultivate a buoyant, joyous sense of the
crowded kindnesses of God in your daily life."
Alexander MacLaren

Work

"Occupation
is the necessary basis
of all enjoyment."

"Sorrow's best antidote is employment."

"I never knew her fail to find happiness wherever she was placed, and good in whomever she came across. Whatever her circumstances might be, they always yielded to her causes for thankfulness, and work to be done with a ready and hopeful heart."

Horatia K. F. Eden

"Cheerfulness is the daughter of employment."

A little more determination,
A little more pluck,
A little more work -- that's 'LUCK'.

Author Unknown

"This is maturity: to be able to stick with a job until it is finished, and to do one's duty without being supervised."

Author Unknown

"Too many people are not faithful in little things. They are not to be absolutely depended upon. They do not always keep their promises. They break engagements. They fail to pay their debts promptly. They come behind time to appointments. They are neglectful and careless in little things. In general they are good people, but their life is honeycombed with small failures. One who can be positively depended upon, who is faithful in the smallest things as well as in the greatest, whose life and character are true through and through, gives out a light in this world which honors Christ and blesses others."

J. R. Miller

Be the labor great or small,
Do it well or not at all.

"Hard work is an accumulation of easy things you didn't do when you should have."

Peace

Plan not, nor scheme, -- but calmly wait;
His choice is best.
While blind and erring is your sight,
His wisdom sees and judges right,
So trust and rest.

Adelaide A. Procter

If peace be in the heart,
The wildest winter storm is full
of solemn beauty,
The midnight lightning-flash but shows
the path of duty;
Each living creature tells some new
and joyous story;
The very trees and stones all catch
a ray of glory,
If peace be in the heart.
Charles F. Richardson

"When you have accomplished your daily task,
go to sleep in peace; God is awake!"
Author Unknown

Drop Thy still dews of quietness,
Till all our strivings cease;
Take from our souls the strain and stress,
And let our ordered lives confess
The beauty of Thy peace!
John Greenleaf Whittier

"The one misery of man is self-will, the one secret of blessedness is the conquest over our own wills. To yield them up to God is rest and peace. What disturbs us in this world is not 'trouble,' but our opposition to trouble. The true source of all that frets and irritates, and wears away our lives, is not in external things, but in the resistance of our wills to the will of God expressed by external things."

Alexander MacLaren

"If I am at war with myself, I can bring little peace to my fellow man."

"My position has come to this ... Am I living near my Saviour? Then I am as happy and peaceful as the day is long, and as light-hearted as a child. It may be that I have plenty of annoyances, but they don't trouble me when His presence is with me. Am I downcast and worried? Then I am away from God."

John Kenneth Mackenzie

I know not, but God knows;
Oh, blessed rest from fear!
All my unfolding days
To Him are plain and clear.
Each anxious, puzzled "Why?"
From doubt or dread that grows,
Finds answer in this thought:
I know not, but He knows.

I see not, but God sees;
Oh, all-sufficient light!
My dark and hidden way
To Him is always bright.
My strained and peering eyes
May close in restful ease,
And I in peace may sleep:
I see not, but He sees.
                              Author Unknown

"In His will is our peace."
                              Alighieri Dante: *Paradiso*

Happiness

"Happiness
is never caused
by circumstances alone."

"The best remedy for discontent is to count our blessings."

Author Unknown

"Happiness ... is nothing else but a perfect conformity, a cheerful and eternal compliance of all the powers of the soul with the will of God."

Samuel Shaw, 1669

"It isn't our position but our disposition that makes us happy."

Author Unknown

"Happiness is good.
The place to be happy is here.
The time to be happy is now.
The way to be happy
is to help make others happy."

"Scorn a pleasure which gives another pain."

"Cheerfulness is health; Melancholy is disease."

"When you have thanked the Lord
for every blessing sent,
but little time will then remain
for murmur or lament."

"If pleasure is the highest aim, it will lead to
unhappiness."

How To Be Happy

Are you almost disgusted with life, little one?
I'll tell you a wonderful trick
To bring you contentment if anything can
Do something for somebody, quick!
Are you awfully tired with play, little one?
Wearied, discouraged, and sick?
I'll tell you the loveliest game in the world,
Do something for somebody, quick!

Author Unknown

Marriage

"What greater thing is there for two human souls than to feel that they are joined for life, to strengthen each other in all labor, to rest on each other in all sorrow, to minister to each other in pain, to be one with each other ... "

From *Adam Bede*, George Eliot

"A wife
doubles a man's pleasures
and divides his cares."

"Marriage is a fusion of two hearts - the union
of two lives - the coming together of two
tributaries, which after being joined in
marriage, will flow in the same channel in the
same direction ... carrying the same burdens of
responsibility and obligation."

Peter Marshall

Home's not merely roof or room,
It needs something to endear it.
Home is where the heart can bloom,
Where there's some kind word to cheer it!
What is home with none to meet,
None to welcome, none to greet us?
Home is sweet, and only sweet,
Where there's one we love to meet us.

Charles Swain

PART II

Stories for Mothers

"Stories are mirrors
in which we are surprised to find ourselves."

'The Sky Pilot', by Ralph Connor, is a story of the Foothills Country in the Rocky Mountains at the turn of the century, when only the ranchers and cowboys of the great cattle ranges and those who were adventurous enough or desperate enough, dared to brave its rigors. To this wild land came a young missionary, college-educated and inexperienced in western ways, and the cowboys called him 'The Sky Pilot'. Gwen was the young daughter of a widowed rancher, the only child among these rough men. Coupled with her kindness to man or beast in trouble, the young girl's courage and skill with horses inspired the loyalty of the hard men. Led by the mysterious aristocrat-turned-cowboy they named The Duke, all of them laughingly yielded to Gwen's imperious will in everything, calling her 'the Little Princess'. And then came Gwen's fall in saving another from harm.

Gwen's Canyon Flowers

As we followed the trail that wound up and into the heart of these rounded hills and ever nearer to the purple mountains, the morning breeze swept down to meet us, bearing a thousand scents, and filling us with its own fresh life.

Through all this mingling beauty of sunlit hills and shady hollows and purple, snow-peaked mountains, we rode with hardly a word, but ever with the thought of the little room where, shut in from all this outside glory, lay Gwen, heart-sore with fretting and longing.

This must have been in The Sky Pilot's mind, for he suddenly held up his horse and burst out:

"Poor Gwen, how she loves all this! -- it is her very life. How can she help fretting the heart out of her? To see this no more!" He flung himself off his bronco and said, as if thinking aloud, "It is too awful! Oh, it is cruel! I don't wonder at her! God help me, what can I say to her?"

He threw himself down upon the grass and turned over on his face. After a few minutes he appealed to me, and his face was sorely troubled.

"How can one go to her? It seems to me sheerest mockery to speak of patience and submission to a wild young thing from whom all this is suddenly snatched forever."

Then he sprang up and we rode hard for an hour, till we came to the mouth of the canyon. As we went down into the cool depths, the spirit of the canyon came to meet us and took The Pilot in its grip. He rode in front, feasting his eyes on all the wonders in that storehouse of beauty.

Trees of many kinds deepened the shadows of the canyon. Over us waved the big elms and around their feet

60

clustered low cedars and hemlocks and balsams, while the rugged oaks and delicate, trembling poplars clung to the rocky sides and clambered up and out to the canyon's sunny lips. Back of all, the great black rocks glistened cool and moist between the parting trees. From many a nook the dainty clematis and columbine shook out their bells, and, lower down, from beds of many-colored moss the late wind-flower and maiden-hair and tiny violet lifted up brave, sweet faces. And through the canyon the Little Swan River sang its song to rocks and flowers and overhanging trees. A cool, sweet, soothing place it was, with all its shades and sounds and silences, and, lest it should be sad to any, the sharp, quick sunbeams danced and laughed down through all its leaves.

No wonder that The Pilot, drawing a deep breath as he touched the prairie sod again, said, "That does me good. It is better at times even than the sunny hills. This was Gwen's best spot."

His face was strong and calm as the hills on a summer morning, and with this face he looked in upon Gwen. It was one of her bad days and one of her bad moods, but like a summer breeze he burst into the little room.

"Oh, Gwen!" he cried, without a word of greeting, much less of commiseration, "we have had such a ride!"

And he spread out the sunlit, round-topped hills before her, till I could feel their very breezes in my face. This The

Duke had never dared to do, fearing to grieve her with pictures of what she should look upon no more.

But, as The Pilot talked, before she knew, Gwen was out again upon her beloved hills, breathing their fresh, sunny air, filling her heart with their delights, till her eyes grew bright and the lines of fretting smoothed out of her face and she forgot her pain. Then, before she could remember, he had her down into the canyon, feasting her heart with its airs and sights and sounds. The black, glistening rocks, tricked out with moss and trailing vines, the great elms, the clematis and columbine hanging from the rocky nooks, and the violets and maiden-hair deep-bedded in their mosses. All this and far more he showed her with a voice so soft and full of music as to fill our hearts with the canyon's mingling sounds. As poor Gwen listened, the rapture of it drew the big tears down her cheeks -- alas! no longer tanned, but white, and for that day at least the dull, dead weariness was lifted from her heart.

The Pilot's first visit to Gwen had been a triumph. But none knew better than he that the fight was still to come, for deep in Gwen's heart were thoughts whose pain made her forget all other.

"Was it God let me fall?" she asked abruptly one day, and The Pilot knew the fight was on; but he only answered, looking fearlessly into her eyes, "Yes, Gwen dear."

"Why did He let me fall?" and her voice was very deliberate.

"I don't know, Gwen dear," said The Pilot steadily. "He knows."

"And does He know I shall never ride again? Does He know how long the days are, and the nights when I can't sleep? Does He know?"

"Yes, Gwen dear," said The Pilot, and the tears were standing in his eyes, though his voice was still steady enough.

"Are you sure He knows?" the voice was painfully intense.

"Listen to me, Gwen," began The Pilot, in great distress, but she cut him short.

"Are you quite sure He knows? Answer me!" she cried, with her old imperiousness.

"Yes, Gwen, He knows all about you."

"Then what do you think of Him, just because He's big and strong, treating a little girl that way?" Then she added, viciously, "I hate Him! I don't care! I hate Him!"

But The Pilot did not wince. I wondered how he would solve that problem that was puzzling, not only Gwen, but her father and The Duke, and all of us -- the *why* of human pain.

"Gwen," said The Pilot, as if changing the subject, "did it hurt to put on the plaster cast for your back?"

63

"You just bet!" said Gwen, lapsing in her English, as The Duke was not present, "it was worse than anything -- awful! They had to straighten me out, you know," and she shuddered at the memory of that pain.

"What a pity your father or The Duke was not here!" said The Pilot, earnestly.

"Why, they were both here!"

"What a cruel shame!" burst out The Pilot. "Don't they care for you any more?"

"Of course they do," said Gwen, indignantly.

"Why didn't they stop the doctors from hurting you so cruelly?"

"Why, they *let* the doctors do it. It is going to help me to sit up and perhaps to walk about a little," answered Gwen, with blue-gray eyes open wide.

"Oh," said The Pilot, "it was very mean to stand by and see you hurt like that."

"Why, you silly," replied Gwen, impatiently, "they want my back to get straight and strong."

"Oh, then they didn't do it just for fun or for nothing?" said The Pilot, innocently.

Gwen gazed at him in amazed and speechless wrath, and he went on, "I mean they love you even though they let you be hurt ... or rather they let the doctors hurt you *because* they loved you and wanted to make you better."

Gwen kept her eyes fixed with curious earnestness

upon his face till the light began to dawn.

"Do you mean," she began slowly, "that though God let me fall, He loves me?"

The Pilot nodded; he could not trust his voice.

"I wonder if that can be true," she said, as if to herself; and soon we said good-by and came away -- The Pilot, limp and voiceless, but I triumphant, for I began to see a little light for Gwen.

But the fight was by no means over; indeed, it was hardly well begun. For when the autumn came, with its misty, purple days, most glorious of all days in the cattle country, the old restlessness came back and the fierce refusal of her lot.

Then came the day of the round-up. Why should she have to stay while all went after the cattle? The Duke would have remained, but she impatiently sent him away. She was weary and heart-sick, and, worst of all, she began to feel that most terrible of burdens, the burden of her life to others. I was much relieved when The Pilot came in, waving a bunch of wild-flowers in his hand.

"I thought they were all gone," he cried. "Where do you think I found them? Right down by the big elm root," and, though he saw by the settled gloom of her face that the storm was coming, he went bravely on picturing the canyon in all the splendor of its autumn dress. But the spell would not work. Her heart was out on the sloping hills, where the cattle were bunching and crowding with tossing heads and rattling horns, and it was in a voice very bitter and impatient that she cried:

"Oh, I am sick of all this! I want to ride! I want to see the cattle and the men and -- and all the things outside."

The Pilot had become cowboy enough to understand the longing that tugged at her heart for one wild race after the calves or steers, but he could only say:

"Wait, Gwen. Try to be patient."

"I am patient; at least I have been patient for two whole months, and it's no use, and I don't believe God cares one bit!"

"Yes, He does, Gwen, more than any of us," replied The Pilot, earnestly.

"No, He does not care," she answered, with angry emphasis, and The Pilot made no reply.

"Perhaps," she went on, hesitatingly, "He's angry because I said I didn't care for Him, you remember? That was very wicked. But don't you think I'm punished nearly enough now? You made me very angry, and I didn't really mean it."

Poor Gwen! God had grown to be very real to her during these weeks of pain, and very terrible. The Pilot looked down a moment into the blue-gray eyes, grown so big and so pitiful, and hurriedly dropping on his knees beside the bed he spoke, in a very unsteady voice.

"Oh, Gwen, Gwen, He's not like that. Don't you remember how Jesus was with the poor sick people? That's what He's like."

"Could Jesus make me well?"

"Yes, Gwen."

"Then why doesn't He?" she asked; and there was no impatience now, but only trembling anxiety as she went on in a timid voice, "I asked Him to, over and over, and said I would wait two months, and now it's more than three. Are you quite sure He hears now?"

She raised herself on her elbow and gazed searchingly into The Pilot's face. I was glad it was not into mine.

As she uttered the words, "Are you quite sure?" one felt that things were in the balance.

I could not help looking at The Pilot with intense anxiety. What would he answer? The Pilot gazed out of the window upon the hills for a few moments. How long the silence seemed!

Then, turning, he looked into the eyes that searched his so steadily and answered simply, "Yes, Gwen, I am quite sure!"

Then, with quick inspiration, he got her mother's Bible and said, "Now, Gwen, try to see it as I read."

But before he read, with the true artist's instinct he created the proper atmosphere. By a few vivid words he made us feel the pathetic loneliness of the Man of Sorrows

67

in His last sad days. Then he read that masterpiece of all tragic picturing, the story of Gethsemane. And as he read we saw it all. The garden and the trees and the sorrow-stricken Man alone with His mysterious agony. We heard the prayer so pathetically submissive and then, for answer, the rabble and the traitor.

Gwen was far too quick to need explanation, and The Pilot only said, "You see, Gwen, God gave nothing but the best -- to His own Son only the best."

"The best? They took Him away, didn't they?"

She knew the story well.

"Yes, but listen." He turned the leaves rapidly and read, "'We see Jesus for the suffering of death crowned with glory and honor.' That is how He got His Kingdom."

Gwen listened, silent but unconvinced, and then said slowly, "But how can this be best for me? I am no use to anyone. It can't be best to just lie here and make them all wait on me, and -- and -- I did want to help daddy -- and -- oh -- I know they will get tired of me! They are getting tired already -- I -- I -- can't help being hateful."

She was by this time sobbing as I had never heard her before -- deep, passionate sobs. Then again The Pilot had an inspiration.

"Now, Gwen," he said severely, "you know we're not as mean as that, and that you are just talking nonsense, every word. Now I'm going to smooth out your red hair and tell you a story."

"It's not red," she cried, between her sobs. This was her sore point.

"It is red as red can be; a beautiful, shining purple red," said The Pilot emphatically, beginning to brush.

"Purple!" cried Gwen, scornfully.

"Yes, I've seen it in the sun, purple. Haven't you?" said The Pilot, appealing to me. "And my story is about the canyon, our canyon, your canyon, down there."

"Is it true?" asked Gwen, already soothed by the cool, quick-moving hands.

"True? It's as true as -- as -- " he glanced round the room, "as the Pilgrim's Progress."

This was satisfactory, and the story went on.

"At first there were no canyons, but only the broad, open prairie. One day the Master of the Prairie, walking out over his great lawns, where were only grasses, asked the Prairie, 'Where are your flowers?' and the Prairie said, 'Master, I have no seeds.' Then he spoke to the birds, and they carried seeds of every kind of flower and strewed them far and wide, and soon the Prairie bloomed with crocuses and roses and buffalo beans and the yellow crowfoot and the wild sunflowers and the red lilies all the summer long. Then the Master came and was well pleased; but he missed the flowers he loved best of all, and he said to the Prairie, 'Where are the clematis and columbine, the sweet violets and wind flowers, and all the ferns and flowering shrubs?" And again he spoke to the birds and again they carried all the seeds and strewed them far and wide. But, again, when the Master came, he could not find the flowers he loved best of all, and he said, 'Where are those, my sweetest flowers?' and the Prairie cried sorrowfully, 'Oh, Master, I cannot keep the flowers, for the winds sweep fiercely, and the sun beats upon my breast, and they wither up and fly away.' Then the Master spoke to the Lightning, and with one swift blow the Lightning cleft the Prairie to the heart. And the Prairie rocked and groaned in agony, and for many a day moaned bitterly over its black, jagged, gaping wound. But the Little Swan poured its waters through the cleft, and carried down deep black mould, and once more the birds carried seeds and strewed them in the canyon. And after a long time the rough rocks were decked out with soft mosses and trailing vines, and all the nooks were hung with clematis and columbine, and great elms lifted their huge tops high up into the sunlight, and down about their feet clustered the low cedars and balsams, and everywhere the violets and wind-flower and maiden-hair grew and bloomed, till the canyon became the Master's place for rest and peace and joy."

The quaint tale was ended, and Gwen lay quiet for some moments, then said gently, "Yes! The canyon flowers are much the best. Tell me what it means."

Then The Pilot read to her, "The fruits -- I'll read 'flowers' -- of the Spirit are love, joy, peace, long-suffering, gentleness, goodness, faith, meekness, self-control, and some of these grow only in the canyon."

"Which are the canyon flowers?" asked Gwen softly, and The Pilot answered:

"Gentleness, meekness, self-control; but though the others -- love, joy, peace -- bloom in the open, yet never with so rich a bloom and so sweet a perfume as in the canyon."

For a long time Gwen lay quite still, and then said wistfully, while her lip trembled, "There are no flowers in my canyon, but only ragged rocks."

"Some day they will bloom, Gwen dear; He will find them, and we, too, shall see them."

Then he said good-by and took me away. He had done his work that day.

We rode through the big gate, down the sloping hill, past the smiling, twinkling little lake, and down again out of the broad sunshine into the shadows and soft lights of the canyon.

As we followed the trail that wound among the elms and cedars, the very air was full of gentle stillness; and as we moved we seemed to feel the touch of loving hands that lingered while they left us, and every flower and tree and vine and shrub and the soft mosses and the deep-bedded ferns whispered, as we passed, of love and peace and joy.

Time passed, and to The Duke it was all a wonder, for as the days shortened outside they brightened inside; and every day, and more and more Gwen's room became the brightest spot in all the house.

One day he asked The Pilot, "What did you do to the Little Princess, and what's all this about the canyon and its flowers?"

The Pilot said, looking into The Duke's eyes, "The fruits of the Spirit are love, peace, long-suffering, gentleness, goodness, faith, meekness, self-control, and some of these are found only in the canyon."

And The Duke, standing up straight, handsome and strong, looked back at The Pilot and said, putting out his hand, "Do you know, I believe you're right, for, of all flowers I have seen, none are fairer or sweeter than those that are waving in Gwen's Canyon."

The End

From 'The Men of the Mountains', by Arthur W. Spaulding
1915

The Sunday Lady

Down in the hills of northern Georgia, just where the Blue Ridge and the Cumberlands halt their invasion of the plains, lies the thriving little city of Rome. Two miles north, on a shady hill, is the proud ancestral home of the Berrys.

Down in one corner of the big oak grove that surrounds it, is a little mud-daubed cabin with a wide stick chimney. It had been the playhouse of the little Berrys, where candy pulls and corn poppings and chestnut roastings had marked many a holiday.

In time, the children of the Berry household grew up, but for one of them the little cabin held memories too hallowed to let it be neglected or forgotten. Martha Berry chose it for her 'den', and with coon skins and bear skins and treasures of field and woods she made it a place to fit the inscription over the fireplace, 'Kyndle Friendship.' The rafters above were hidden behind festoons of peppers and popcorn ears, and outside by the door hung the cedar water pail and the gourd dipper. Over in one corner was a little old rosewood melodeon, shaky of leg, and with keys yellow from age. Here Martha Berry spent many and many a quiet hour with her books and the wild things of the woods that visited her.

One balmy Sunday afternoon in April, three other little wild things crept up to the cabin, and through some unchinked cracks stood peering in at this wondrous palace of beauty, and at the lady who lived there.

Miss Berry, suddenly conscious of the scrutiny, looked up from her book to encounter the three pairs of gray-blue eyes surveying her paradise with such wonder.

"Come in," she called to them.

But the three little barefoot, ragged children shrank away in fear. Going to the door, Miss Berry tried to talk with them, but it was only when she held out the temptation of bright red apples that she could persuade them to enter.

Then, remembering that it was Sunday, she began to tell them Bible stories. These were all new to them, as she learned when she asked them questions about the stories.

"Don't know," they said, "don't know. Hain't never been to no Sunday school. We'uns' Hardshells."

"Do you have any brothers and sisters?" she asked.

"I got about eight," said one.

"I got about ten," said another.

They were children of tenant farmers nearby, men from the mountains, or kin to them.

She asked them to return next Sunday and to bring their brothers and sisters.

In the busy activities of the week that followed, Martha Berry nearly forgot her promise. The next Sunday she was sitting with some city visitors on the gallery of the 'big house', when she saw a procession coming through the woods. Not only children were coming, but men, women, babies and dogs. Excusing herself, she hurried down to meet the delegation.

Quickly forming an impromptu program in her mind, she said, "First we'll sing something."

The wheezy little melodeon was wondrous to the amazed ears of the eager children, who pressed around it as they sang to Miss Berry's 'lining out', "I am so glad that Jesus loves me."

And then she told them Bible stories, stories so new and fresh to these neglected 'Hardshells' that not only the children, but the father and mothers, sat with rapt faces.

Every succeeding Sunday brought more and more visitors, some with gifts of shuck mats for seats for the growing audience, which filled the cabin and overflowed into the grove.

The Sunday school grew. People came, rain or shine, and soon Miss Berry had to invest a hundred dollars in lumber, and the men and boys of the Sunday school put up a small schoolhouse to which they soon had to add a little room in front, and then a big room on the back.

Then some of the members moved up to Possum Trot Creek, and they sent word begging Miss Berry to come and open a Sunday school there. So she drove the eight miles and held Sunday school with them in an old, dilapidated house that had survived the war.

One Sunday it rained, and though she fled from corner to corner, she was soaked before the Sunday school and the shower were over. So she asked the people to put on a new roof before the next Sunday.

"But it might not rain for a whole month," one man protested.

"Yes," said Miss Berry, "but it might rain next Sunday!"

She pointed to an oak tree nearby which would make good 'boards', and told the men if they would cut it up and shingle the roof she would bring the nails and treat the workers to lemonade. They came, and she came, and probably most important of all, the lemonade came. It was an unaccustomed drink to them, but it was highly appreciated by all, even the old man who remarked with a chuckle that he "never heard of a woman a'bossin' of a house-roofin' before."

From Possum Trot "the Sunday Lady," as the countryside affectionately began to call her, was soon extending her chain of Sunday schools in other directions, with her sister and others enlisted as helpers.

Only the angels and the heavenly Father know the far-reaching changes wrought for Eternity by that one little lady who sat in her cabin that first day, reading and enjoying her Sunday 'rest'. How many of us would have called the children in? When the visitors continued to come and multiply, how many of us would have gracefully withdrawn on about the seventh Sunday? How many would have found the hot summer good reason to end an undertaking that threatened their leisure and limited their social activities? How many would have found the long wagon ride, or the leaking roof, sufficient excuse to decline the plea from 'Possum Trot'?

But not Martha Berry.

A Voice had said, "Whom shall I send? and who will go for us?"

And out of her leisurely, sheltered life she came, replying, "Here am I ... send me."

The End

Louisa May Alcott's tale of four sisters did not end with the book 'Little Women', but continued in 'Little Men', which told of the school 'Jo' established at Plumfield with her husband, Professor Bhaer. Their pupils included the twins of Jo's sister Meg, and various needy children who came to them one by one from lives of difficulty. Dan was an orphan boy from the city streets, earning his living by selling papers. At fourteen, he was a little older than the others, and he came to Plumfield when Nat, another boy they had taken in, innocently told Dan "how nice it was there, and why didn't he come live there, too?" Gruff and impatient of any restraint, Dan wreaked havoc, leading the boys into scrape after scrape, and finally setting the house afire in a forbidden night escapade. Reluctantly, the Bhaers sent him to a farm where difficult boys were often helped.

Mrs. Jo's Mother-Heart

"My poor Dan! I never can quite forgive myself for letting him go," sighed Mrs. Jo.

At the sound of the name, little Teddy, who had never forgotten his friend, struggled down from his father's arms, and trotted to the door, looked out over the sunny lawn with a wistful face, saying, "My Danny's tummin' soon."

"I really think we ought to have kept him, if only for Teddy's sake. He was so fond of Dan, and perhaps a baby's love would have done for him what we failed to do."

"I've sometimes felt that myself. But after keeping the boys in a ferment, and nearly burning up the whole family, I thought it safer to remove the fire-brand, for a time at least," said Mr. Bhaer.

July had come, and haying begun. The house stood open from morning till night, and the lads lived out of doors, except at school-time.

One balmy night when the little lads were in bed, and Mrs. Bhaer undressing Teddy in her parlor, he suddenly cried out, "Oh, my Danny!" and pointed to the window, where the moon shone brightly.

"No, lovey, he is not there, it was the pretty moon," said his mother.

"No, no, Danny at a window. Teddy saw him," persisted the baby, much excited.

"It might have been," Mrs. Jo thought, and hurried to the window, hoping it would prove true. She called Dan's name, then ran to the front door with Teddy in his little shirt, and made him call too, thinking the baby voice might have more effect than her own.

No one answered, and they went back much disappointed. Teddy kept popping up his head from the crib to ask if Danny was not "tummin soon". By and by he fell asleep, the lads trooped to bed, and the house grew still. Mrs. Jo sat sewing and thinking of the lost boy.

It was past ten when she rose to shut up the house. As she paused a minute to enjoy the lovely scene from the steps, something white caught her eye on one of the haycocks scattered over the lawn. The children had been playing there all afternoon, and fancying that one had left a hat, she went out to get it. But as she approached, she saw that it was neither hat nor handkerchief, but a shirt sleeve with a brown hand sticking out of it. She hurried round the haycock, and there lay Dan, fast asleep.

Ragged, dirty, thin, and worn-out he looked; one foot was bare, the other tied up in the old gingham jacket which he had taken from his own back to use as a clumsy bandage for some hurt. He sighed and muttered as if his dreams disturbed him, and once when he moved, he groaned as if in pain, but still slept on quite spent with weariness.

"He must not lie here," said Mrs. Jo, and stooping over him she gently called his name.

He opened his eyes and looked at her, as if she were a part of his dream, for he smiled and said drowsily, "Mother Bhaer, I've come home."

The look, the words, touched her very much, and she put her hand under his head to lift him up, saying in her cordial way, "I thought you would, and I'm so glad to see you, Dan."

He seemed to wake thoroughly then, and started up looking about as if he suddenly remembered where he was.

His face changed, and he said in his old rough way, "I was going off in the morning. I only stopped to peek in, as I went by."

"But why not come in, Dan? Didn't you hear us call you? Teddy saw, and cried for you."

"Didn't suppose you'd let me in," he said, fumbling with a little bundle which he had taken up as if going.

"Try and see," was all Mrs. Bhaer answered, holding out her hand and pointing to the door, where the light shone hospitably.

With a long breath, as if a load was off his mind, Dan began to limp towards the house, but stopped suddenly.

"Mr. Bhaer won't like it. I ran away from Page."

"He knows it, and was sorry, but it will make no difference. Are you lame?" asked Mrs. Jo as he limped on again.

"Getting over a wall a stone fell on my foot and smashed it. I don't mind," and he did his best to hide the pain each step cost him.

Mrs. Bhaer helped him into her own room and once there, he dropped into a chair, and laid his head back, white and faint with weariness and suffering.

"My poor Dan! Drink this, and then eat a little. You are home now, and Mother Bhaer will take good care of you."

He only looked up at her with eyes full of gratitude, and then began slowly to eat the food she brought him.

"Where have you been, Dan?" she asked, beginning to get out some bandages.

"I ran off more'n a month ago. Page was good enough, but too strict. I didn't like it, so I cut away down the river with a man who was going in his boat. I worked a couple of weeks with a farmer, but I thrashed his boy, and the old man thrashed me, so I ran off again and walked here."

"How did you live? It was a long, long tramp for a boy like you."

"Oh, I got on well enough, till I hurt my foot. Folks gave me things to eat, and I slept in barns and tramped by day."

"But if you didn't mean to come in and stay with us, what were you going to do?"

"I thought I'd like to see Teddy again, and you. And then I was going back to my old work in the city, only I was so tired I went to sleep on the hay. I'd have been gone in the morning, if you hadn't found me."

"Are you sorry I did?" Mrs. Jo looked at him half - merrily, half-reproachfully, as she knelt down to see his wounded foot.

The color came up into Dan's face, and he kept his eyes fixed on his plate as he said very low, "No, ma'am, I'm glad.

82

I wanted to stay, but I was afraid you -- "

He did not finish, for Mrs. Bhaer interrupted him by an exclamation of pity when she saw his foot, for it was seriously hurt.

"Mr. Bhaer must see and dress it at once," and Mrs. Jo hurried into the next room, leaving the door ajar behind her, so that Dan heard all that passed.

"Fritz, that boy has come back."

"Who? Dan?"

"Yes, Teddy saw him at the window, and we called to him, but he went away and hid behind the haycocks on the lawn. I found him there just now fast asleep, and half dead with weariness and pain. He ran away from Page a month ago, and has been making his way to us ever since. He pretends that he didn't mean to let us see him, but go on to the city and his old work, after a look at us. It is evident, however, that the hope of being taken in has led him here through everything, and there he is, waiting to know if you will forgive and take him back."

"Did he say so?"

"His eyes did, and when I waked him, he said, like a lost child, 'Mother Bhaer, I've come home.' I hadn't the heart to scold him, and just took him in like a poor little black sheep come back to the fold. I may keep him, Fritz?"

"Of course you may! This proves to me that we have a hold on the boy's heart, and I would no more send him away now than I would my own Teddy."

Dan heard a soft little sound, as if Mrs. Jo thanked her husband without words, and in the instant's silence that followed, two great tears that had slowly gathered in the boy's eyes brimmed over and rolled down his dusty cheeks. No one saw them, for he brushed them hastily away, but in that little pause the soft spot in his heart was touched, and he felt an impetuous desire to prove himself worthy of the love and pity that was so patient and forgiving. He said nothing, he only wished the wish with all his might, resolved to try in his blind boyish way, and sealed his resolution with the tears which neither pain, fatigue, nor loneliness had been able to wring from him.

"Come and see his foot. I am afraid it's badly hurt, for he has kept on three days through heat and dust, with nothing but water and an old jacket to bind it up with. I tell you, Fritz, that boy is a brave lad, and will make a fine man yet."

"I hope so, for your sake, my dear. Your faith deserves success. Now I will see your little Spartan. Where is he?"

"In my room. But, dear, you'll be very kind to him, no matter how gruff he seems. I am sure that is the way to conquer him. He won't bear sternness nor much restraint, but a soft word and infinite patience will lead him as they used to lead me."

"As if you were ever like this little rascal!"

"I was in spirit, though I showed it in a different way. I seem to know by instinct how he feels, to understand what will win and touch him, and to sympathize with his temptations and faults. I am glad I do, for it will help me to help him, and if I can make a good man of this wild boy, it will be the best work of my life!"

"God bless the work, and help the worker!"

Mr. Bhaer spoke now as earnestly as she had done, and both came in together to find Dan's head down on his arm, as if he was overcome with sleep. But he looked up quickly and tried to rise as Mr. Bhaer said pleasantly, "So you like Plumfield better than Page's farm. Well, let us see if we can get on more comfortably this time than we did before."

"Thank you, sir," said Dan, trying not to be gruff, and finding it easier than he expected.

"Now the foot! Ach! This is not well. We must have Dr. Firth tomorrow. Warm water, Jo, and old linen."

Mr. Bhaer bathed and bound up the wounded foot, while Mrs. Jo prepared the only empty bed in the house. When it was ready, Mr. Bhaer took the boy in his arms and carried him in, helped him undress, laid him on the little white bed, and left him with another hand-shake and a fatherly, "Good-night, my son."

Dan dropped asleep at once, and slept heavily for several hours. Then his foot began to throb and ache, and he awoke to toss about uneasily, trying not to groan, for he *was* a brave lad, and did bear pain like "a little Spartan".

Mrs. Jo had a way of flitting about the house at night, to shut the windows if the wind grew chilly, to draw the blankets over Teddy, or look after Tommy, who occasionally walked in his sleep. The least noise waked her, and her quick ear caught the sound of Dan's little moans, and she was up in a minute.

"Are you in pain, Dan?"

"It's pretty bad, but I didn't mean to wake you."

"I'm a sort of owl, always flying about at night. Yes, your foot is like fire. The bandages must be wet again."

"Oh, that's *so* good!" sighed Dan, as the wet bandages went on again, and a long drink of water cooled his throat.

"There now, sleep your best, and don't be frightened if you see me again, for I'll slip down by and by and give your bandages another sprinkle."

As she spoke, Mrs. Jo stooped to turn the pillow, when to her great surprise, Dan put his arm round her neck, drew her face down to his, and kissed her, with a broken "Thank you, ma'am," which said more than the most eloquent speech could have done, for the hasty kiss, the muttered words, meant, "I'm sorry, I will try."

She understood it, accepted the unspoken confession, and did not spoil it by any token of surprise. She only remembered that he had no mother, kissed the brown cheek half hidden on the pillow, as if he were ashamed of that little touch of tenderness, and left him, saying what he long remembered, "You are my boy now, and if you choose, you can make me proud and glad to say so."

The next day was Sunday, and the house was so still that he didn't wake till near noon, and looking round him, saw an eager little face peering in at the door. He held out his arms, and Teddy tore across the room to cast himself bodily upon the bed, shouting, "My Danny's tum!"

Then came the doctor, and the poor Spartan had a bad time of it, for some of the little bones of his foot had to be put to rights, and great drops stood on his forehead, though he never cried out, and only held Mrs. Jo's hand so tight that it was red long afterwards.

"You must keep this boy quiet, for a week at least, and not let him put his foot to the ground. By that time, I shall know whether he may hop a little with a crutch," said Dr. Firth.

"It will get well sometime, won't it?" Dan asked, looking alarmed at the word 'crutches'.

"I hope so," and with that the doctor departed, leaving Dan much depressed, for the loss of a foot is a dreadful calamity to an active boy.

"Don't be troubled, I am a good nurse, and we will have you tramping about as well as ever in a month," said Mrs. Jo, taking a hopeful view of the case.

But the fear of being lame haunted Dan, and even

Teddy's chatters did not cheer him, so Mrs. Jo proposed that one or two of the boys should come in and pay him a little visit, and asked whom he would like to see.

"Nat and Demi. I'd like my hat too. There's something in it I guess they'd like to see."

Mrs. Jo brought him his old straw hat stuck full of butterflies and beetles, and a handkerchief containing a collection of odd things picked up on his way: birds' eggs, carefully done up in moss, curious shells and stones, bits of fungus, and several little crabs, in a state of great indignation at their imprisonment.

To the boys, Dan related his adventures much more fully than he had done to the Bhaers. Then he displayed his 'plunder', and described each article so well that Mrs. Jo, who had retired to the next room to leave them free, was surprised and interested.

"How much the lad knows of these things! I am glad to find out this taste of his. It is a good one, and may perhaps prove the making of him. If he should turn out a great naturalist, I should have cause to be proud of this year's work," and Mrs. Jo smiled as she built castles in the air, just as she used to do when a girl, only then they were for herself, and now they were for other people, which is perhaps the reason that some of them came to pass in reality -- for charity is an excellent foundation to build anything upon.

So interested were the boys that Mr. Bhaer had to come himself to tell Nat and Demi it was time for the walk. Dan looked so wistful, that Father Bhaer carried him to the sofa in the parlour for a little change of air and scene. Mrs. Jo sat near by, showing Teddy pictures, and she nodded toward the treasures still in Dan's hands.

"Where did you learn so much about these things?"

"I always liked 'em, but didn't know much till Mr. Hyde told me."

"Who was Mr. Hyde?"

"Oh, he was a man who lived round in the woods studying these things -- I don't know what you call him -- and wrote about frogs, and fishes, and so on. He stayed at Page's, and used to want me to go and help him, and it was great fun."

"I think you were so fond of going with Mr. Hyde, you rather neglected Mr. Page," said Mrs. Jo slyly.

"Yes, I did. I hated to have to weed and hoe when I might be tramping around with Mr. Hyde. Page thought such things silly, and called Mr. Hyde crazy because he'd lay hours watching a trout or a bird."

"Suppose you say *lie* instead of *lay*, it is better grammar," said Mrs. Jo gently. "Yes, Page is a thorough farmer, and would not understand that a naturalist's work was just as interesting, and perhaps just as important as his own. Now, Dan, if you really love these things, as I think you do, and I am glad to see it, you shall have time to study them, and books to help you. But I want you to do something besides, and to do it faithfully, else you will be sorry by and by, and find that you have got to begin again."

"Yes, ma'am," said Dan meekly, and looked a little scared by the serious tone of the last remarks, for he hated books, yet had evidently made up his mind to study anything she proposed.

"Do you see that cabinet with twelve drawers in it? Don't you think those drawers would be good places to put your eggs, and stones, and shells, and lichens?"

"Oh, splendid, but you wouldn't like my things 'clutterin' round', as Mr. Page used to say, would you?" cried Dan.

"I like litter of that sort. And if I didn't, I should give you the drawers anyway, because I have a regard for children's little treasures, and think they should be treated respectfully. Now, I am going to make a bargain with you, Dan, and I hope you will keep it honorably. Here are twelve good-sized drawers, one for each month of the year, and they shall be yours as fast as you can earn them, by doing the little duties that belong to you. I believe in rewards of a certain kind, especially for young folks. They help us along, and though we may begin by being good for the sake of the reward, if it is rightly used we shall learn to love goodness for itself."

"Do *you* have 'em?" asked Dan, looking as if this was new talk for him.

"Yes, indeed! I haven't learnt to get on without them yet. My rewards are not drawers, or presents, or holidays, but they are things which I like as much as you do the others. The good behavior and success of my boys is one of the rewards I love best, and I work for it as I want you to work for your cabinet. Do what you dislike, and do it well, and you get two rewards -- one, the prize you see and hold; the other, the satisfactions of a duty cheerfully performed. Do you understand that?"

"Yes, ma'am."

"We all need these little helps, so you shall try to do your lessons and your work, play kindly with all the boys, and use your holidays well -- and if you bring me a good report, or if I see and know it without words -- for I'm quick to spy out the good efforts of my boys -- you shall have a compartment in the drawer for your treasures. Shall we do this, Dan?"

The boy answered with one of the looks which said much, for it showed that he felt and understood her wish and words, although he did not know how to express his interest and gratitude for such care and kindness. She understood.

"Now, let us begin by putting those nice beetles in a safe place. These compartments will hold a good deal, you see."

"But I can't go out to find any new things," said Dan, looking piteously at his foot.

"I dare say the boys will bring you loads of things."

"They don't know the right sort. Besides, if I lay, no, *lie* here all the time, I can't work and study, and earn my drawers."

"There are plenty of lessons you can learn lying there, and several little jobs of work you can do for me."

"Can I?" and Dan looked both surprised and pleased.

"You can learn to be patient and cheerful in spite of pain and no play. You can amuse Teddy for me, read to me when I sew, and do many things without hurting your foot, which will make the days pass quickly, and not be wasted ones."

Here Demi ran in with a great butterfly in one hand, and a very ugly little toad in the other.

Dan laughed at the toad, and said he had no place to put him, but the butterfly was a beauty, and if Mrs. Jo would give him the materials, he would put it right in the drawer.

"I know how to do it -- Mr. Hyde taught me."

Dan gently poured a drop of camphor on the insect's head, the pale green wings fluttered an instant, and then grew still.

This was hardly over when Teddy shouted from the bedroom, "Oh, the little trabs are out!"

Demi and his aunt ran to the rescue and found Teddy dancing excitedly in a chair, while two little crabs were scuttling about the floor.

"I'll have to let these fellers go, for I can't keep 'em in the house," Dan said, with evident regret.

"I'll take care of them for you, if you will tell me how, and they can live in my turtle-tank just as well as not," said Demi, and he bore them away.

"What a good boy he is!" said Dan, remembering that Demi had given up his walk to bring him the butterfly.

"He ought to be, for a great deal has been done to make him so."

"He's had folks to tell him things, and to help him. I haven't," said Dan, with a sigh, thinking of his neglected childhood, a thing he seldom did, and feeling as if he had not had fair play somehow.

"I know it, dear, but you shall have all the help that we can give you now, and I hope to teach you how to help yourself in the best way. Have you forgotten what Father Bhaer told you when you were here before, about wanting to be good, and asking God to help you?"

"No, ma'am," very low.

"Do you try that way still?"

"No, ma'am," lower still.

"Will you do it every night to please me?"

"Yes, ma'am," very soberly.

93

"I shall depend on it, and I think I shall know if you are faithful to your promise, for these things always show to people who believe in them, though not a word is said."

Mr. Bhaer carried Dan away to his bed early, and Teddy came in his pajamas to say good night.

"I want to say my prayers to Danny. May I?" he asked, and when his mother said "Yes," the little fellow knelt down by Dan's bed, and folding his chubby hands, prayed softly.

"Pease Dod bess everybody, and hep me to be dood."

He left smiling sleepily over his mother's shoulder.

But after the evening talk was done, the evening song sung, and the house grew still with Sunday silence, Dan lay in his pleasant room wide awake, thinking new thoughts, feeling new hopes and desires stirring inhis boyish heart, for two good angels had entered in. Love and gratitude began the work which time and effort were to finish, and with an earnest wish to keep his first promise, Dan folded his hands together in the darkness, and softly whispered Teddy's little prayer:

"Please, God, bless everyone, and help me to be good."

The End